Ben Shafran, born in Israel, immigrated to the US as a young teenager. He worked his way through architecture school at CCNY, graduating as an architect, and has made the New York area his home ever since.

He spent the COVID lockdown period in the Berkshires at his country home in Hillsdale, NY, which is the setting and inspiration for many of the nature poems in this volume. It was during this period that he first started writing poetry, writing his first poem as a personal take on Psalm 1, responding to a challenge, and has been writing poetry steadily since.

To Jake and Ewi for all their help and support.
To R. Sharon Kleinbaum for inspiring the journey.

Ben Shafran

DEAR READER

AUSTIN MACAULEY PUBLISHERS™

LONDON • CAMBRIDGE • NEW YORK • SHARJAH

Ordering Information
Quantity sales: Special discounts are available on quantity purchases by corporations, associations, and others. For details, contact the publisher at the address below.

Publisher's Cataloging-in-Publication data
Shafran, Ben
Dear Reader

ISBN 9798891551985 (Paperback)
ISBN 9798891551992 (ePub e-book)

Library of Congress Control Number: 2023922830

www.austinmacauley.com/us

First Published 2024
Austin Macauley Publishers LLC
40 Wall Street, 33rd Floor, Suite 3302
New York, NY 10005
USA

mail-usa@austinmacauley.com
+1 (646) 5125767

Table of Contents

Dear Reader

We are partners you and I
I write you decipher
I unburden and you puzzle.
Often quite often intention
and perception have no
connection but each in
its way is equally true
at the moment of
interaction for the words
are no longer my
possession. Once scribed
they are born to 'twine
with any willing passing eye

Introduction

Simple Tales

The words are fancy
And sentiments high
When poems on
Pages are scribed

But tales of the world
Are anything but
And lives simple and complex
And humdrum abound.

We decry injustice
And ennoble the meek
While ignoring the banal
As though it didn't exist.

And it's all well & good
To extoll all the best
But it's in everyday stuff
Where the magic dwells.

The changing of seasons
The lives of small wildlife
The movements in heaven
Or sudden creative sparks.

The life of the farmer
Working the land
Dependent on weather
And markets capricious.

The bus driver making
His rounds midst
Traffic and turmoil
Ending his shift with enormous relief.

Or the clerk bleary-eyed
Confronting his screen with
its urgent requests
Piling up in endless streams.

These are examples
Of the simplest of tales,
This is the stuff
I wish my poems could tell.

But alas no teller of
Tales am I, only the
Scrivener for my eyes.

So humbly I offer recorded
Herein their intake of nature
And follies of man.

Forever preserved
As I had perceived.

Scribblings

Surely This Is a Joke

The Rabbi said write…
And obediently I write.
The Rabbi said your take…
And unbeckoned out they pour
Feelings suppressed longings denied
Rush out tumbling like waters from Moses' rock.
Dancing in the sunlight
Evaporating in the heat
Not quenching the thirst.

The Poem

You are evanescent
You do not exist
You are the wide-mouthed amphora
Receiving my heart's pour.
Unflinching and unjudging
Not rebuking nor supporting.
Your silence is the balm
Calming my heart.

Lament for a Lost Poem

Where in heavens name did you go?
You were so real
Title opening lines and all.
Last night you came
As pre-dream revelation
And I in too much pain
Did not heed your call
Did not jot you down.
Now in the light
Of a new dawn
You've gone missing, mocking
My inaction with open derision.

Write

I want to write more
But can't.
I want the release
And joy
Of free-flowing words
But they're out
Of reach.
Bottled up inside,
Guts tied up in knots,
Confused and distracted
I search in vain
For inspiration,
For the solace
Of the polished phrase.

Problem is
It's not the words;
The ideas that
Scaffold the words
Have all taken a walk,
And without the core
What use are the words?

Gobbledygook and Gibberish

Evil twins born to Adam & Eve
The day they partook of that apple,
Who then survived the Flood
As figureheads of Noah's Ark
And built the Tower of Babel.
From whence their progeny
Spread to every known language
Bedeviling multitudes of writers
And quickly becoming
The lingua franca of all orators.
Gave birth to Alternate Facts
Myriads of syntax mistakes
And beloved aphorisms
Such as "It ain't over till it's over."
And with this, this mishmash
Handywork of Brother Gibberish
Is most definitely done and over.

The Language of Poetry

Circumlocution allusion delicacy
no direct engagement
fear of mundanely engaging
the mundane lest it be
deemed unworthily common
so we sail our sea
fearful of approaching any shore
avoiding shoals of easy intelligibility.

That's one version.

Another, accords the delicacy
magical evocation of emotions
unobtainable with the direct
banal and commonplace
imagery to soar the soul
impart delight to parsed phrases.

Maybe.

One version more,
we simply want
the words to dance
to spin for joy.

What, Me Worry?

(Self-admonition)

What, me worry? Why?
The words don't rhyme
Who says they should?
The tales are crooked
So what? Don't know
The end? That's the point
Let it unfold as it wants
Let the end surprise
And beguile you.
Let go of that angst
The journey and sights
Are the important parts.
Play with the words
Switch the syntax
Savor the syllables
Aren't they just delicious?
So write something
For goodness' sake
Enjoy the process
Man and relax!

Poetic Delights

In the perplexity of twisted
intertwined tangled words
traipsing on the tongue
like *Times'* crossword clues,
plain as day
mysterious as twilight,
lie provocative thoughts
expressed in delectable
phrases all to be had
for trifling efforts.

A Conversation

Am I talking to you? Am
I reaching you?
Listening to your silent
Voice? Writing as though
We are sitting in
A caffe conversing?
Am I?

The Wonder of the Poems

"God is in the details"
Declared Mies the God
And it's details I picked on.
They are the components
The tell-tale marks
That explode into the big.

A lifetime of details
Accumulated unawares,
like a lake behind a dam
Bursting in overflowing stream
Hurriedly writing themselves here
Before they disappear.

In Nature's Realm

The Wind Knows Not
Where It Goes[*]

The wind knows not where it goes
the wind knows naught but it flows
over ocean over hill over dale over river
mighty hurricane or gentle zephyr
welcomed relief from scorching days
fearsome adversary on ocean's waves
the wind knows not where it goes
but everywhere it blows it blows.

---

[*] *Jose Saramago, The Gospel According to Jesus Christ*

Ode to Spring

Pan is dancing on my electronic page
Imaginary Putti take wing
A scarlet cardinal alighted on Old Maple
And timid azure is sneaking a peek.

Can hope be far behind? ...Joy?

Moonrise

Our bedroom window faces south
A large "Picture Window."
Sunshine and clouds
Swaying trees and deer
Burst through, each in their time.

Before spring gathers strength
Before trees wear their mantle
The rising moon can be glimpsed
Hiding behind the massive trunks
Playing Peek-a-Boo with the night.

Spring

Sprung like a released coil of steel
Spring is suddenly here
Sub-freezing at dawn
Mid-seventies in the afternoon
Red-headed Finches
Appearing at birdfeeders
Robins strutting the lawn
And day lilies breaking loam
All messengers
Of coming warmth.
The blue of the sky
Turns milky with haze
The winds strengthen pace
And yet are welcome
As harbingers of brighter days
Houses empty streets hum
And hearts are filled
With sheer delight and cheer

Sunset

The sun is setting.
I have no view of the great Orb,
But framed in the window
Old Maple's branches
Are suddenly all a pinkish glow.

My dismay heightens with
The speed of change
From bright spring day
To melancholy night.

While tomorrow another day
Awaits I can't help mourning
Now the passing of today.

Spring Snow

Old Maple
Last eve all aglow
Is now covered
With fresh fallen snow.

Slowly drifting flakes
Covering the lawn
Turned bright spring eve
Into winter's morn.

But spring it is
And come bright day
All this white
Will be swept away.

The Robin

Once before she built a nest
On the sconce outside the door.
Ever since, each spring
I wage a war discouraging repeat.
This year the robin won.
The price is my presence
At will on the porch
Interrupting her repose
Each time I approach
And sending her to flight.

She is however quite clever,
And will strut on the path
In front of the porch
Demanding her right of return.
Her insistence is so great
That I generally relent
And vacate my seat
To make way for the bird.

In consequence of which
Little robins appear
Beaks agape
Clamoring to be fed.
Now, when I sit on the porch
Mother Robin has
A new approach.
Despite my presence
And braving elemental
Fear she now flies
On to the nest
Right past my seat,
Wrigglies hanging from her beak
Manna for the hungry progeny.

Distant Thunder

A cliché, a book, or a movie title
Can't remember which,
Attention grabbing nonetheless
When nature insists.
Low ominous rumble
Starting afar from the side
Rolling overhead
Ever so slightly louder
To die distantly softly
On the other side.

Heralded by darkening
Skies, trees at a standstill,
Birds alert,
And not a zephyr to be felt.
A storm is surely coming
Or maybe not.
This midsummer weather
Is hard to predict
And nature's fickleness
Is plainly linked.

Swallows

My favorite avian
Blue gray and white
Swift agile and light
Somersaulting in air
Turning on a dime
Chasing life and having fun.

Cardinals

We're having a surfeit
Of them this year.
Bright scarlet
On wing and grass.
Catching the eye
Not letting go.
Begging the question
Which came first
Office or bird?

Flight

My brother pilots his planes
Says they love so
To take to the air.
Bernoulli explained
The how and the why
Which still fails to dispel
The magic and beauty
Of gulls gliding above waves,
Of raptors riding high thermals,
Of silvery wings
Sleek and majestic
On contrails of vapors.
And I, despite my age
I don't much care,
And often stop to stare
At wings on air
Careless and free.

To Jake

A Walk in the Time of Pandemic

Two miles
One mile uphill one mile down.
Glorious nature Bucolic
Rolling hills Pastures Plowed fields Woods.
The make-believe relief
Of forced coronavirus isolation.

Life has come to a halt for humans.
But spring is not to be tamed
Not for him social distancing from summer.
Flowers bloom birds appear green shoots
Gifts from mocking gods.

Thus it has always been and forever be.
And the walk?
A cruel reminder of imminent mortality.

April 12, 2020
Hillsdale, NY

The Bear

Coffee early morning
Out of the woods
A black bear comes
Ambling leisurely body rolling
Like a ship in a cross seaway
Aiming for the bird feeder
Not even three feet away.
With powerful paws
He bends it earthward
Enough to comfortably sit
And leisurely consume the seeds.
That done, he slowly
Ambles back to the woods
Whence he emerged
Utterly nonplused.

Stillness

Utter stillness reigned today
On daily jaunt.
Clouds a high ceiling,
Leaden light,
Magnified magical space.

Not a creature in sight
From hillcrest to hillcrest.
Not a sound,
Save scattered songbirds
And a lonely crow.

Communing with silence
For entirety of walk.
Sharpened senses
Register freshening wind,
Foreshadowing coming storm.

On a Summer Day

The steely-gray river under
Low-hanging clouds
of a midsummer scorcher
burst momentarily
into joyful play when
the sun peering through
a gash in the clouds shed
silver confetti sparkling
like polished diamonds
on a patch of the river.
The shifting shrapnel
pieces coalesced, forging
a shimmering scepter
from the far bank
to my window, when Helios
fled its confines.
A ravishing vanishing
fit for Neptune royal gift.

Quickening pace,
the caravan
of night advanced
led by the moon[*]
and in her train
bats stars fireflies
crickets and tree frogs.
All was tranquil
As in early creation.
Trees merged becoming
blacker black patches
on a black curtain
shimmering as satin by starlight.
Moonflowers' giant white trumpets,
stages fit for Oberon
and Titania's madcap revels,
shed intoxicating fragrance.
A fox trotted along
the road disappearing
in the undergrowth.
Languor prevailing
endowed the night
With blissful magic.

____

Naguib Mahfouz, Children of Gebelaawi

The Storm

It was raining all day today
Strong country rain.
The wind unenclosed
Free to roam whipped
The old towering pines.

As they shook and swayed
Like congregants in prayer
Some, tiring of the struggle
Snapped sprouting wounds
Of raw fresh timber.

Ancient creatures that they
Are wise in the ways of the wind
Their newer branches
Already claiming victory
And proclaiming perseverance.

Fireflies

Like notes of
The Lark Ascending
They spiral
Higher and higher
Seemingly suspended
By invisible wires.
An earthly mirror
Of the starry night.

Highlighted against
The velvet black
Of midsummer darkness
They flash intermittent
Neon yellow-green
Keeping pace with
The strobe of the plane
High in the firmaments.

Deep silence reigns.

Only the dance of the fireflies
Enlivens a tranquil night.

Dawn, Summer Solstice

Slumber time still, deep into
what would be the darkest
part of a winter night, the sky
has a tinge of light. Barely,
but brightening rapidly; propelling
the quiet city to quicken pace.

Dawn, Winter

Dawn of a winter's morn
Cloudless skies highlight
Crests of the hills
Discerned as
A thin sharp pencil line
Drawn by a master
On a blank piece of paper,
Black below barely lighter above.

Summer Nights

Darkness mellowed the heavy oppressiveness
of a summer day in the city.
A passing zephyr caressed us and sweetened
our urgent kisses
on a park bench in the playground under
rustling sycamore leaves
filtering the streetlamp light. The urban oasis
provided a salon for
our youthful explorations of the gifts of Aphrodite.
The magic lingered
and though faded by the passing of the years
decades later in old age
a drive under a tree-filtered city streetlight
sparked the memory alive,
on another summer's night.

Intimations of Autumn

The days are still very hot
And summer in full force
But the fogy mornings
Already herald fall.
The swallows and the
Red-winged blackbirds
Denizens of the fields
Have disappeared.
Crickets chirp softly
Not yet in chorus
In the cool dewy grass.
The deer graze in packs
And the young
Of the turkey rafters
Have taken to wing.
There is an edge
To the breeze
A melancholy note
Disappearing quickly
When sunshine breaks.
Red-tinged leaves
Not yet dominating
The scene
Are still absorbing
The warmth of the

Lower-on-the-horizon sun
In futile attempt
To restore their youth.
Fall will surely come
It can't be stopped
But I hope to God
Not for a long time.

Birds on a Wire

When the morning fog
Has lifted
When the sun has
Crested the hilltops
And the air is steeping
In its warmth
You can find
The swallows
Lining the roadside wires
Soaking up the new day.
And if you should
Chance to pass by
Underneath
They'll lift up in
A great big cloud
Fleeting hither
And tither in
Great somersaults
Only to settle on the same
Spot after you pass.

The Bobcat

We almost collided.
He coming out
Of the woods
Trodding a well-worn
Deer track,
I walking along
The road heading
Home a mere
Few paces on.

Both stopped, equidistant
From the intersection
Of our paths staring
Warily at the other
Cautious but not afraid.
The inevitable of
Our era, post modern
Meeting primordial.

Both regaining ease
He nonchalantly
Hightailed his
Way back along
The trail turned
Once for a parting
Shot and merged
With the shade.

Autumn Once Removed

I am not going to tell you
About the flaming-red maple
Next to the canary-yellow ash
Up on the hill visible from here.
What would be the point?
No doubt by now you have read
Countless poems extolling autumn's beauty
And one more paean isn't going
To extend your emotional perception,
And besides I am not good at description.
Nor am I going to tell you
About the fragrant fall air
Redolent with the smoke of burning wood.
That would be like trying to
Describe a color to the blind.
After all you are not here to
Breathe a sample so whatever
Your perceptions are, they
Most certainly are not of this air.
But I can tell you that autumn is here
And Thanksgiving is near.
Trees are shedding their mantle
The brown leaves rustle as you walk through
Them making a pleasing sound.
The days still trend warm
Indian summer has not turned its back
But the cool nights requiring fire
And flannels or sweaters
Are harbingers of snowed-in nights to come.

This is farm country.
The hay lies about in great
Big rolls in the still green fields
Waiting to be gathered.
The corn has been harvested
Leaving brown stubble behind
Next spring to be plowed under.
The fields are abounding with
Large rafters of wild turkeys
Feasting on the fallen grain,
The deer are visibly changing color
From summer beige to winter gray
And this year in particular
There is an abundant crop of nuts
Littering the roads
Manna for everyone: ravens, squirrels,
Chipmunks and all manner of wildlife
Fattening up before dearth comes.
I do hope you get the picture
Snug in your corner,
And unlike me
Not dreading the dead of winter.

Ladybug

She landed with a
Thud on my table,
Fell off the wall.
Exhausted and famished
Having been inside a
House closed for the cold.
She lay there motionless
A very long time
Eventually summoning
Enough strength to cling
to a core of an apple
I laid by her side.
For several days she barcly moved
Never getting off that core.
Slowly she regained vitality
And for a couple of days more
She thoroughly explored that core.
One evening she climbed
Off her apple and
Ranged all over my table.
First slowly and then
At a gallop. Her tour
Led her to the computer
Where upon a flicker
Of light she took fright
And flew off to God knows where
Never to be seen again.

Here We Go Again

Gray overcast turned sun to cold white disc
And north winds sweeping over dirty-beige fields
Combined to magnify cold of early winter
Intermixed with autumn's lingering dregs.
Lawns still green, verdant highlights
In world turned deathly-gray
Fail to dispel depression, mocking need.
How will next months be endured?
How will wherewithal of will be rallied?

December

The air is chill
Wind at standstill
Only movement
To be seen
Are tiny flakes
Falling down straight.
Thin new
Ground cover
Let's grass tips
Poke through
But covers the driveway
With fresh coat
Of plaster like snow.
Silence reigns
Under low clouds
Soft as fleece
Gray as steel.
Snow in
Middle distance
Hovers like fog
Catching white reflections
Off the ground
And brightening up.
This scene will repeat
Countless times
Till to the rescue
Springtime comes.

What Shall We Do About Winter?

What shall we do about winter he asked
As though we had any power at all
To belay its onset. The solstice arrived today,
Very punctually, riding the geodesic of spacetime
Carved by the sun in the eternal sky
And will now climb higher to summer.

That is the answer to winter's problem
Climb aboard and ride it higher
All the way to spring and summer.

Robins on Christmas

They're supposed to be way south
where the earth is soft and the air warm.
Yet here they are on this most
frigid of Christmases fleeting about
my window zealously chasing others
from imaginary turf on the frozen ground.
Nary a worm to be had from this
concrete earth which perhaps explains
their unusual intolerance.
Yet the starlings all around belie
the dearth of sustenance
confirmed by the bright red
Winterberries scattered in abundance.

At Twilight

In mid-winter at twilight the other day
A herd of deer gathered in our garden
Not even ten yards away.
It was at that time
When remnants of day just barely linger on
But the fullness of night has not yet begun.
A circular early-evening moon crested the hills
And shed soft gauzy light on the unfolding scene.
The deer appearing like luminous gray velvet
Against the darkening skies
Just kept coming on and on.
The initial group of four
Was soon joined by two more
And two more again and then by some more
'Till congregated there were close to a score.
Young and old all mixed together drifted
By ones and twos to the field across the road
'Till the last one bounding with grace
Over a dormant bush
Disappeared into the frigid gloom
Leaving not a trace.

Winter Blues

Abounding leitmotifs
Of silence dormancy
Or absence
And whipping
Winds coming off
The ponds or the
Tops of the hills
Biting into the skin
Invigorating some
Tormenting others.
Gray twilights
Descending all too early and
Daylight rising all too late
Even with the screwed
Up clock.
Pretty snow
Turning to slush
Gathering mud
And looking yuck.
I wish I wish
I wish in vain
I wish for spring
To come again,
No! Not in springtime damnit
But right now. Today!

Tropical Evening

The ceaseless motion of the ocean
Slowly came to a stop
Everything was still
Halcyon winds heralded sunset
A lone whale breached the
Smooth surface of the bay and disappeared
Twilight was stealthily approaching
Turning turquoise to blue
And blue to indigo.
The universe was holding its breath.
Waiting… For what?

A Month or So

Just one more month
Just make it through
The short month February
And March will wink
Its promise of
Warmth renewed life.
Swallows will appear
Then robins. The blue
Of the skies will lose its
Intensity soften up
And become hazy.
Green shoots will appear
And then flowers.

Just one more month!

Winter's End

The ambient air is cool
the sun in the gaps
between the scudding
white cotton-ball clouds
sends waves of warmth
counterbalancing the breeze
caressing body & soul.
Stems of the rose bushes
are now green and though
it's still February tiny green
leaves flecked with red edges
are budding adding to the
promises of life awakening
bestowed by the sprouting
bulbs. Wood doves paired
up are gently cooing and
the robins are back. Spring
in its fullness is just around
the corner riding
the shoulders of the
coming winter storm.

Intimation of Spring

The deer trudge slowly
After the long winter
Visibly depleted of energy.
They seek their provender
Above the snow cover
Eating growth they normally loath.
But a small flock of bluebirds
Appeared today
And a few swallows
Were again hanging
On the wires
The snow cover is thinning
The stalks of the
Wild roses are greening
And the days are sensually longer
Hinting of mirth and warmth
And life awakening.

Just around the corner.

Gulls

Crooked wings motionless
on swift invisible winds
soaring high skimming
the water still motionless

as though they invented
flight to torment gravity.
Thieves snatching morsels
from others with loud

nonchalance brazenly
claiming rights rather
than continuing the hunt
the hardship of which

belied by the ease
of the glide to a precise
spot at the right instance
to snatch a hapless fry.

Musings

Vibrations of Love

Vibrations of love
thrill of love sonnets
intensity of color fields
wild poppies after winter rains

exquisite proportions of the Parthenon
discoveries upon sonata development
primordial staccato of the *Bolero* drum
or sublime repose of the *Moonlight.*

Shall I keep going? But you're already
familiar with it all. So how do you
explain it for I cannot. How does it
happen… the transport of the soul?

Dig In

Dig in.

Dig in deep
Dig into the past
Dig into your soul
Dig into the memories
So the short future
Might be full.

Don't let go
Don't skip
Don't erase
Don't retreat
Don't despair
And don't resist.

Confront it all
Own it all
Love it all
And let it all
Be your guide
To yourself!
If I am not for me
Who will be?

Joy

Walking on sunshine
the slanted beams bouncing
to my steps as piano keys
respond to finger strokes
sending heavenward bound
unsounded sweet melodies
singing of Alegria wrapped
in happiness and grace.

To Mary Joyce

Heads

Marie Antoinette lost her pretty head
It now lay in a basket and was colored red.
She had not kept her head
When matters in France came to a head
And offered cake instead of bread
Incensing the crowd to shout "off with her head."

Had her queenship not gone to her head
Had she kept a proper cool head
Had she sought advice when she was in over her head
When she couldn't make head nor tail
    of the brewing, stewing matters coming to a head
She could have remained queen and kept her head.

Memories

Come, show yourselves
Don't hide don't be shy,
After all we are one
You and I.

Where have you gone
All these years?
Where did you rest?
Why didn't you say hello
Or call home for a chat?
Your presence is needed now
Before it's too late,
Come, please come
Before we both expire.

Come, show yourselves
Tell me a story
Lull me to sleep
Remind me of feelings
Long dormant
Deliberately buried
Foreclosing the absence
Of rejected beauty
From aching so deeply.

Triptych of a Marriage

(A Ballad)

1st Panel. At First

As twilight approached, his favorite hour,
The light softened. She alighted from the
Cab, regal in a swirling cape all charcoal and black.
Taller than he expected strikingly arresting.

A dazzling smile broke out on her face
As they introduced themselves. The smile
That to this day makes his heart skip
Several beats each time it appears.

Drinks turned to dinner; time stretched
Unnoticed as they skimmed their lives.
Perhaps it was not love at first sight
But the attraction was lasting and immediate.
He did not foresee then nor could he
The conflicts that will arise based on their pasts.

2nd Panel Blinkered

He did not rebel or shout or throw tantrums
He blended with the background
And closed the emotional spigot.
Closed it so tight it slipped his mind
He completely forgot it was there.
Which doesn't mean it disappeared,
Only that it was hidden and unattended,
Building up a reservoir of thwarted needs
Suppressed desires and wishes.

That was OK. Conscious life was easier to cope
With that way, as long as he lived in his own cocoon.
Then they met and he didn't know how to unspool
That tightly woven cocoon, free himself to reach
Out to her be equal with her.
Despite loving her deeply he found himself
Unable to fully get her desires
As she desired them and adept to them.
That hidden reservoir had but a single command:
Do Not Agree or Submit! That, became his rebellion!
  And she,   they,   bore the brunt.

3rd Panel to Her

He wanted her to know
That even though
They came to an end
Even though
They did not succeed
It never was because his
Love diminished.
The more time passed
The more it grew
The more he longed for her,
For the soft touch
Of her lips the evanescent
Fragility of their hugs
The erotic charge
Of her ever more
Beautiful visage.

Had he been more aware
More demanding
Of his needs more outspoken
Perhaps they would
Have been more
Even keeled and had
A fighting chance.
Alas he couldn't remake
The past. All
That was left was to tell her
so she knew,
How much he
Still adored her.

What Were You Like

What were you really like
When I was growing up?
What ticked under that carapace?
Clearly you had some strength.
When still young you
left home and hearth.
You ventured out. You pursued
Culture in an impoverished place.
Where books were precious
And rare you had a library
For Pete's sake!

I felt sorry for you and sad
Seeing you wearing blue
Once on Shabbat.
Was that because we were too
Poor for you to wear white?
Or were you making
A fashion statement
In your own unique bent?

You had no buddies
But I do remember a friend,
He drove us multiple
Times in his truck.
Why did that contact
Come to an end? Or
Did it? You never let on.
When in company, always family,
You did if memory serves, converse.
So why so aloof and silent with us?

What were you really like?

Original Sin Reimagined

Primordial Eve told my
firebrand feminist friend
that we had it wrong all along.
Pre-dawn she came and whispered
"There never was any sin at all!"

"'Sin' is so English," she said, "which
anyway no one spoke until our progeny
abandoned the Tower of Babel.
In our tongue we simply said
(S)he missed the mark.

"Bowmanship bungled, permitted
to be corrected. And if
it was seriously serious than
a line was crossed, but 'sin'?
For that you're dammed forever

"and as you can plainly see
you guys are anything but.
No no there was no sin
this is a coming-of-age story,
how we, Adam & me, grew up.

"We were young adults then
albeit only a couple of hours old
with hormones coursing

and devil-may-care attitude
which, wouldn't you know, conjured a devil

"masquerading as a slithering
snake talking with a forked tongue,
which he really did have, and reassuring
me with utmost sincerity
of the magic mushroom quality of that tree.

"And you know what? He was right!
Taking my fate in my hands I had visions
of the starkness of life, of the toil & turmoil
so far removed from the leisure of the Garden
of Pleasure in that oh-so-young world."

"Rather than frightened, I was delighted
by the augured power the vision implied
of limitless choices and control over
success and progress; of the deep
guile to guide men, possessed by us sisters.

"I quickly got Adam just as high, and his vision
being congruent with mine, we hurriedly
left that place to enjoy the pleasures of
sex hard work creativity and most
of all the freedom of responsibility."

Raise the Lintels

After the imagery of Psalm 24:7

GOD does not play dice
Declared Albert the Great
But he was wrong.
The universe
Never immutable
Always changing
Forever follows
Quirky quantum laws.
Unintelligible but
Knowable affording
Humans a shadow
Of a glimpse
Into Divine domains.
Spacetime immense
Is to the Divine but a speck
Raise the lintels high
To let Divinity in.
In, to the innermost soul
To the core
Wherein Godly
Impulses sojourn.
Raise the lintels high
Higher than you dare.

America

(A song of an immigrant)

1957 Chevrolets newly minted
Bobby Sox and Elvis
Rock'n'roll ascendant.
The Shiny City on the Hill
In a world, war weary still.

Quonset huts at Idlewild
Wooden shacks (can't call them houses) in Queens
Dung-colored apartment blocks
Can this really be the reality of the dream
The embodiment of the goal?

In time it sinks in,
This is different.
Different in scope and scale
Different in attitude and manner
Proud confident strong
Unselfconscious at all.

Energized for perpetual advancement
She seeps into your blood
Coerces your love.

That Face in the Mirror

A lifetime of looks in the mirror
Young combing hair shaving when older.
Daily encounter with that face in the frame
Never altering always the same.
And then, one day out of the blue
A silent question pops, is that really you?
How does this face comport
With that face, twenty years old?

Enigma

My mother.
Except for a few
Faded photos
All else is imaginary.
No one transmitted
Her memory
Least of all my father.
They all spoke fondly of her
Except my father,
Who never spoke
Of her at all.
But none ever told
Anything of substance.
Little bits here and there
Unconnected unrelated
Illuminating nothing at all.
And I, I never thought to ask
The most obvious
Question of all;
As everyone has a mother
Where is mine?
Growing up
I did not want to know
What I didn't know
And now that I do
There is no one left

Who knew.
All that's left are
Faded photos
Burning questions
And imagination.

(27 Sivan, the Hebrew calendar date on which she gave birth
to me 77 years ago)

Riff on PSALM 6:6

*"For there is no praise of You among the dead; In Sheol,
who can acclaim You?"*

Down to Hades went Orpheus
To bring back Eurydice.
Hades being Greek
Where anything mythical is probable,
He virtually succeeded.

Sheol on the other hand
Is serious stuff,
It is positively the last stop.
The doors snap shut
And nothing ever escapes.
A veritable Black Hole
Of prayer memory and hope.

Question begged:
Why would the LORD
Originate death
If prayers and praises
Are his wants and desires?

Life

B.P. says
(Being a biologist,
He should know)
That death
Is the price of the ticket
To be admitted to life.
The most precious
Possession
In the universe
Has a ticket price.
Imagine that!

The Talmud says
You are born
Like it or not
And you will die
like it or not.
Of course the
Sages of the Talmud
Not familiar
With Darwin
Were just reiterating
Evident evidence.

And then
There is Nature.
And Nature
In utter silence
Says nothing. She
Just goes about
Her business
Sowing death
As she pleases
And bringing
Life joy love
And happiness
As she pleases.

Prayer

After Mary Oliver

The lowliest of objects
Weeds in cracked pavement
For example are as
Worthy subject for plain
Words of focused observation
As any uttered Hosanna.
Kadesh, Sanctus, Quds
Mater to the utterer
Rather than the Eternal
And trading favors is
A losing proposition.
Ah! But numinous wonder
At flourishing life
Or transcendent beauty
From wherever it comes
Seeping in beguiling
Soul, in these the power of
Prayer dwells.

Something from Nothing

The great divide
Of the human mind,
Whence comes all this?
A quantum field fluctuation
Or Divine fiat?
Both sides envision
Metaphorical bolts of lightning
Hurled out of Nothing
Or eternal preexisting Something.
Which stumps either side;
Wherefrom did the Nothing
Or the Something arise?

Original Sin Tradition

The tale is full of questions
inconsistencies and contradictions
yet tradition has it as divinely
told, which renders the above
irrelevant but not beyond
the human mind. Hence
the myriad jump-through-hoop
explanations and exegetical
explorations of a magical
foundational moment.

Adults, only a few hours old
beautiful beyond beauty
sharing all divine attributes
and not even demigods, humans
as we, immodestly curious
assertive of self heedless
of strife courting danger.
The Eternal envious
of his like-us handiwork.

And it's all well and good
until it's not when divinely
bestowed free-will is
exercised and the Divine
finds that to be an insult.
Creation was the expression of His
need for relation and here
He is encountering opposition
and for all eternity the die
is cast in any relation the self is first.

Canaan Now

I ascend the hill where the old mosque stands in Jaffa
Terminus of the Roman road climbing from the depth of the
Jordan
Valley at Jericho through the lunar landscape of the Judean
desert and on
To the heights of eternal stone-encrusted Jerusalem then
descending to
The sea the ancients called The Middle of the Earth. The
sparkling port
So alive in the sunshine diverts my sight further on to the dense
Glass skyscrapers of Tel-Aviv founded as a suburb on the sand
dunes
And now vibrant and thriving surpassing all expectations.

On his last day alive did Moses see all this from the heights of
Mt Nebo?
Did Joshua reach as far as this coast when he subjugated this
land?
And Jesus when walking in Galilee or descending to its sea
Did he notice the blood-red poppies covering the hills after
the winter rains reminders of all the blood shed in this land?
Did King David rule here as well? And Herod the Great
Builder of luxurious Caesarea further north did he embark here
At this old port still alive and functioning albeit now only for
fishing?

After passage of millennia now a steady flow of jets stream-in
From the sea banking low over traffic-clogged highways where
Camel caravans once trod narrow dusty paths and crusaders fought.
Where in this tiny land with outsized history did Saladin evictor
Of Richard the Lionhearted pitch his tent? What marvelous
Modern contraption now occupies that spot? Civilizations
Long gone thrived here leaving their marks layer upon layer to the
Depths of foggy history and then disappeared. Will we thus disappear
As well our marks the highways and runways and power towers?

Kaddish

(Sanctification)

Kaddish is our prayer
For the departed.
In ancient Aramaic
And not a word
Pertaining to death.
A holy Magnificat,
A hymn sanctifying God!
"Yit'gadal Ve'yitkadash
Shem'ei Rabbah…"
May the Great Name
Be Magnified and Sanctified…

In the middle
Of my tenth summer,
In Old Ashkelon
Thousands of years old
Philistine city
Turned Arab village
Turned Israeli town
In the heat of the day
Outside the synagogue
While playing near
A hedgerow of brisling cactus
And ripening figs
My father informed me
In dispassionate words
Of the death long ago

Of a mother I never knew
Nor knew about
As he at no time had
Spoken of her before
Nor ever again after.
I am old enough – he said
To recite the Kaddish – he said
In her memory – he said
A memory I did not possess.
Offering neither
Explanations nor comfort
Not inquiring
About feelings.

Incomprehension
And confusion
Turned to shame
At suddenly finding
Myself an orphan
The only motherless
Child around
The only child
Reciting the Kaddish
Among congregation
Of grownups.
That feeling while
Losing its sting
As the years passed
Never fully abated
And when in time
I disengaged
From the faith

I stopped repeating
This annual event.
The shock of
The experience
Foreclosed for me
Open inquiry into
This new revelation.

God and mother
Were soon forgotten
Inconsequential uninteresting
Not effecting
Progress or ambition
Until in old age
I hit a wall
And further denial was
Not an option.
Once again in
The middle of summer
Awareness of her
Reality became palpable
Forcing thoughts
To the by now
No longer knowable,
Requiring acknowledgement
Recognition acceptance,
Leading me to cast off
My constricting chains
Join a Shabbat service
Around the anniversary

Of her death
And in her memory
The memory I
Do not possess
I once again
Recited the Kaddish.

May I be at peace.

A Portrait of God

(A short history of God)

Inspired by Psalm 11

In his image he created him
With nostrils flaring in anger,
Anger easily aroused,
Sitting or standing or striding
Hands raised to smite
Or elevate and
Periodic regrets.

In his own likeness he created
Him in the beginning,
With head hands
Feet eyelids and genitalia.
Of stone clay wood or metal
To ward off terrifying
Impenetrable nature

And then when matured
He relegated him
To the transcendence.
Out of eyesight
And into the imagination
Where, in the human soul
All Godly attributes abide.
In his image.

David and William

Riff on Psalm 30:12 and Richard III

David: "Hafa'<u>h</u>ta mis'pedi lema'<u>h</u>ol"
                -You turned my mourning to dancing-

William   "Now is the winter of our discontent
                Made glorious summer by this sun of York;
                And all the clouds that lour'd upon our house
                In the deep bosom of the ocean buried.
                …Our stern alarums changed to merry meetings,
                Our dreadful marches to delightful measures."

Oh William, really? too many words.
Surely you were familiar with David,
You couldn't best him
For brevity and beauty?
And you thought you're the master.
For shame!

Not that we don't quote you almost as frequently
And not that you didn't have in mind
"La gente paga, e rider vuole qua."
-People pay and they want to lough-
Being an impresario after all
The box had to be paramount.
Still, if Anna Russell could do
Richard's entire Ring in twenty

Minutes instead of twenty hours
Couldn't lame Richard have hurried up?
Maybe then he wouldn't have had
To trade his kingdom for a horse.
Some lousy deal maker he was!
Didn't he read *The Art of the Deal*?
David never had to do that
And he was as big a schemer as Richard
When it came down to wives.

Oh, William William William
I am truly disappointed!

Swimming

Swimmers doing the backstroke
Toward a waterfall[*]
In hindsight my life
Oblivious to surroundings
Consequences future
Inviting disaster to strike
And so it did, repeatedly.

---

[*] *Viet Thanh Nguyen, The Sympathizer*

Whence Does Beauty Originate

whence does beauty originate
what alarms her slumbers wake
how pliant she in originators'
conjuring hands malleable her
shape-shifting dance once
thundering with strength
once sinewy with grace
the soul & breath of consciousness

What If

A passing comment from A.
About an exchange with J.
Set my mind adrift, thinking

What if…

What if she hadn't died when I was one,
What if she had lived to eighty-one,
What would I have then become?
Just as I am today, or more open and free?

What if she just then did not depart
how would he have fared?
Capable and loving or silent and sad
As later he appeared to me.

That I was loved and cherished
Every faded photo confirms,
But what if we had grown together
How would we then have been?
Close and loving or jaundiced and irritating?

What if later on she was still around
When his livelihood the war destroyed,
Would they have then grown closer yet
Or drifted and become estranged?

And what if she had not passed on
Would there then have been others?
Certainly not my actual brothers,
They had come much later on.

******

Useless speculations?
Waste of time?
But what if, instead,
Sharpened life perceptions?

The Awakening

Slowly unfolding like a lotus flower opening,
arms outstretched, hands twirling in
gentle movements as in a Hindu dance.
Grace descending to awake the dawn
trailing in her wake happiness and joy
to crown the newly born morn.

To Mary Joyce

Original Sin Delusions

So he came down to be tortured
and crucified *for what*??
To amend the insult to *Dad*?

UPPITY ADAM & EVE WISHING TO GROW
AND KNOW INSULT INSECURE ALMIGHTY RAIDING
HIS LARDER. O, what headlines they garnered!

Slow to anger I am but it's been millennia plus.
Enough of nostrils flaring in wrath,
time to settle accounts by Jove! But how?

Oh, I know, l'll pull an Abraham, sacrifice
my only begotten son, begotten not made, mind you.
That'll learn you to misbehave you little miscreants,

how dare you want to know as much as I?
Seeing as you've always been a stiff-necked
lot, starting with your original forebears

on that first ever Friday (O, why couldn't
they have just left quietly for the weekend?)
I now challenge you to a life/death struggle.

Oh no, not your death, you're already
mortal. My death is what's required,
not a deicide but a Dei-Suicide.

And the return on investment?
Your everlasting salvation my little darlings.
Now isn't that a deal; you sin, I die, you win.

-'ey! Who's the wise guy who thought this up?
Me?
Really?

Over the Cemetery Wall

Her grave is but five
Paces from the wall
Of an old peaceful
Shady cemetery in the
Heart of the busy
Vibrant city that grew
And surrounded it.
I was already an old
Man at my first visit
Decades after her death
In my infancy.
Alone in that tranquil place
I stood silently
Contemplating her name
Graved on the grave.
Sadness welling and for
The first-time mourning
I started uncontrollably crying
Until a dim sound from
Over the cemetery wall
Slowly growing louder
In my awareness
Broke through the flood:
The sound of children playing.
That most joyous of all sounds
Offered soothing comfort
And put a smile on my face
Before I departed that place.

Could It Be?

Mesopotamia resurgent is
vying yet again with the lower desert potentates
for the cradle of civilization.
Four millennia gone in a blink of an eye
center of gravity long shifted west
way west but this perpetual strife
is still news central. Assur Babylon
and Persia vs. Egypt and Arabia.
The center of the gyre hasn't
shifted one bit, players
of successive waves dead
but not the avarice & greed.

Knowledge

1

"Knowing thyself" or something similar
The great Socrates declared,
"Is the beginning of knowledge."
Behold! Facts do not Knowledge constitute,
But unobscured inner light does!
No veils shirking or denial
Only laser-focused inner gaze.
For then, and only then,
Can true truth be known.

2

But what to make of events?
What to make of *Rashomon*,
The Alexandria Quartet or
Trump's "alternate facts"?
Arguing that Knowledge
Is unknowable and
Purely subjective. And if so,
What to make of the rule of law?

A Requiem

There was the time when a boss of mine relayed
his agony on the event of turning thirty.
I could not share in his misery as I remembered
his remarks when it was my turn to turn tricenary.

If anything at all it was a nonevent as I recall.
We all were young sophisticates then
urbanites bent on conquering the world
careers to race young families to raise.

None wasted any time examining the passage
of time or marked its progress except to revel
in its repetitive celebratory events: the birthdays
holidays dinner parties and children's progress.

And so the years passed uncounted unremarked
while children middle aged became and we
remained the same still young if not quite in limb
most certainly in heart. Not for us the doddering lassitude.

And then once upon a sunny early-spring day
while taking my place at a local park-bench
a group of boys passed by. Thirty something
boys full of chatter life and lightness.

And a piercing thought then crossed my mind;
are they us? Is that how young and foolish and
happy and inconsequential were we? And will they
someday question it all in a more or less similar way?

A Lion Roars/Who Fears Not? [*]

Where have you gone to Fear?
Why have you averted your face?
Am I not worthy of your presence
no longer a worth-while prize?
A life led in your worship
and you turn out to have
feet of clay wings of lead
and the patience of a passing
breath. Fie on your head
remain banished deepen exile!

---

[*] *Amos 3:8*

Original Sin Legacy

Death was set free
with that first bite,
hitherto only a potential
virtual nonexistent

it now was liberated
to roam the globe
at will and gather back
the ultimate prize

free-willed no longer
immortal Soul.
Fragile though she is she
is jealous of her liberty

won't easily submit
to marauding Death
and he in turn absolutely
won't ever be caged

again and so the match
was set: the Finite End
with no End v. Soaring
Grand Magnificence.

A Draft

It was a point of pride
a source of merriment
amongst us youngsters
each time we heard our
elders mutter "Please
close that…there is a draft."

Oh how I long for those
days each time I now
sit on a park bench
the winds off the river
encountering my back.

The Sound of Silence

"…and the sound of utter silence shall be heard…"[*]

Zephyrs whispering softly
dancing among the pines
climbing the mountain slope
above the finca, gently tinkling
bells on grazing goats,
sloshing in the agricultural pond.
The sounds of silence
no susurrous traffic no words.
Silence.

[*] *From the traditional Rosh Hashana Service*

Stories

(Despair)

What if the stories we tell ourselves
don't get resolved, what if these stories
of greed avarice cruelty and indifference
are who we are, are our true selves
and the other stories of community
charity beauty are fleeting evanescent myths?

What if our all-too-short golden age
was an aberration arising of outside forces
forced on our tumultuous existence
petering out when danger lifted letting
us slide back to our default state of
selfishness tribalism ignorance and strife?

What if our foundational myths
were brought forth to cover
the discomfort arising from awful
intentions deliberately pursued
no longer capable of being hidden
from the prying eyes of conscious thought?

And what if it has always been thus
and whatever progress we can
be proud of is spread over
time spans beyond generational
awareness, forever leaving the living
mired in strife and distress?

On Being Human

You can dream of being the best
of rising to the top of the heap
ideas originating as though heaven sent.
You can dream of excitement propelling
forward, forward to the apex
of your dream remaining when awaked.
Or you can dream of dolce-far-niente
lotus grazing or anything in between.
Choose life! The Eternal commended
and indeed life is all choices. Now what?

Blood and Glory

1870. Guerra Guerra Guerra,[*]
ignoring the blood and gore
Verdi extols the glory.

Meanwhile up north
the Franks & Goths
are busily spilling blood aplenty.

Obeying gravity
blood to earth returns
and to the Gods shouts mightily

or so at least
would have us believe
God Almighty.[*]

Do we really need his testimony
when our own eyes
can plainly discern the story?

Or can they?
What on earth have we
for millennia seen is war's glory?

---

[*] Aida, act 1
[*] Genesis 4:10

Dead

Not a care nor worry.
No feelings no desires
No beguiling or tormenting hope.
No problems either!
Dead!
As dead as "Might as well be a doornail."
But I ain't doornail
I am rotting flesh
On which earth is thrown.
Will I taste the loam?
Will I taste of the loam?
Will unendurable claustrophobia set?
This end has no end.

Musings on Original Sin

Adam to Eve & Eve to the snake.
From primordial memory
from first stories
from the very beginning
courage is lacking.

It wasn't an apple; that fruit is benign
it was knowledge
which caused the decline
in moral composure
and growth of denial.

Equally true and just as disturbing
are the credit grabbing
all too facile
kowtowing
know-nothings

Who never partook
of the fruit of that tree
acquired no knowledge
yet for others' accomplishments
are hungrily grasping.

Who then is accursed?
We or that tree
which in exchange
of its produce commands
innocence to surrender.

Are knowledge and
innocence so mutually
exclusive and did
God so create them
for his amusements?

Did he deliberately stick
his leg in the aisle
hoping for stumble?
Else why did he plant
those two damned saplings?

Just asking!

******

Lots of questions creation creates
but the ones for me paramount are these:
had Adam & Eve eaten first
the fruit of the other tree
would we have all like gods become
and act as obnoxiously as the original one?
Or better still are we in fact the original one?

Idyll Idealized

Grandma Moses had a method
primitivity elevated. The heck
with fluff or visual correctness
but the visually inspiring, ah, that
was a worthwhile preserve.
Emotional journeys through
prospects of memory evoking
a pre-industrialized Eden.
Green pastures white winters
blue waters, landscapes
of contentment and bliss.

I Am of the West

I am of the West
I know not the East
its merits as they are
are beyond my ken.
But of the West even if
only for selfishness' sake,
for I need an upswell
to rise and succeed,
'love thy neighbor' I do discern.

I am of the West
and claim morality's staff
I hold a baton generationally
passed from the deserts of Sinai
and Arabia through Rome and Sevilla.
Proudly I proclaim my
inheritance my allegiance
all while heartlessly
I watch refugees perish.

I watch them drown in mighty waters
as once I watched Pharaoh's
hosts I watch despair
I watch death throes
smugly I watch until it's too late
not a twinge of sorrow
furrows my brow not
a shadow of doubt
penetrates my heart.

The Green Jacket

Twice she now passed
ambling by and twice
I silently remarked upon
that kelly-green jacket design.

Though the color was becoming
there was nothing remarkable
about the garment's appearance,
nothing that is except the jolt

to my memory. A pre-teen in
an impoverished land
wearing with sheer delight
a jacket in style so similar.

And that clasp, oh my,
this is the first one I've seen
since that oh so very long ago
nearly seven decades or so.

Change

Sure everything changes everything
moves on but are there no speed limits?
What used to be an acceptable pace
has now transmuted to a hyper-velocity race.

As I can claim just one conscious life
that's all the span I can comment on
but from my youth to my dotage now
nothing is even remotely along the same furrow.

It used to be strictly verboten, that is
if one was even minimally cultured,
to use a noun as a verb or the reverse but now
more and more the two are casually melded.

Digital is now taken for granted yet
it wasn't all that long ago that analog
was boss and the reigning aesthetic
was the brute power of the iron horse.

And though supersonic travel has now ceased
yet the remotest corner of the globe remains
a mere hop jump and a skip, whereas in the not-too-distant
past a sail to Europe's shores was at least five days.

Fedoras gave way to shaved heads, ties and
jackets to open chests, formals to jeans,
miniskirts have come and gone and come again
and now transparent dresses are taken for granted.

And it's actually all well and good, for the flux
is the force that thrusts life, but how does one
whose attention span is long gone keep up
with all the changes going on?

The Problem of Old

Must old men be dominated by the past?
Can nothing new come before that
final goodbye? With all that experience
under the belt can no more dots
be connected for creative spark
to catch on? Why is it that it is
the young with no experience
to fall on who always innovate?

Habits congealed? Good-old-days
nostalgia? Unconscious fear
of the consequence of failure so far
removed from the conscious of the young?
Must old men be confined to ruminate
upon the past? Life does go on until
it's not, so why give up exuberance and drive?
"Rage on…" he wrote and whyever not?

Exceptional Men
Disrupt the Peace

And we don't want that don't like that
equanimity and status quo is what's
desired prejudices unchallenged.
But exceptional men pay no mind
and in a celestial *Whack-a-Mole* game
pop up and disrupt here
and there ultimately everywhere
leaving us mortals to catch up.
Our fury rising rising unconsciously
at our unperceived unacknowledged
hated mediocrities we lash out
and for a while just a little
while bury the exceptional.

Original Sin Motivation

His charge was negative
refrain from acting
that's it no more
which tested his ego

how could he he with
the free will be constrained
circumscribed commanded
so much for "in his image"

but it wasn't rebellion
on the contrary
the action was devotional
a sacrifice

of his immortality for his love
of the Ineffable.
I can do better than the charge
I can do more

I can demonstrate my
devotion more intensely more visibly
by transgressing this once,
and sacrificing my soul for the sake of the love.

My Ode to Joy

After the closing verse of the last and most joyous of the
Psalms (150:6)
"Every breathing being shall exalt the Lord"

Schiller I am not
And David I am not
Neither am I Beethoven
How then
Can I, mortal,
Add to the cacophonous
Chorus of joy
Heavenward bound?

The crickets' choir at night
The bullfrog in the pond
The chirp of the swallows
And the caw of the crows
And the cry of the gulls
All rising to heaven
Like notes from the tower of Babel.

What can my contribution be?
I can't dance like Zorba,
What elation I feel
Is all internal,
What's my addition
To the sum of creation?

******

May my words true and sincere
Be an acceptable substitute.